Greetings California!

H.S.P. CALIFORNIA EXCURSIONS

It takes you there!

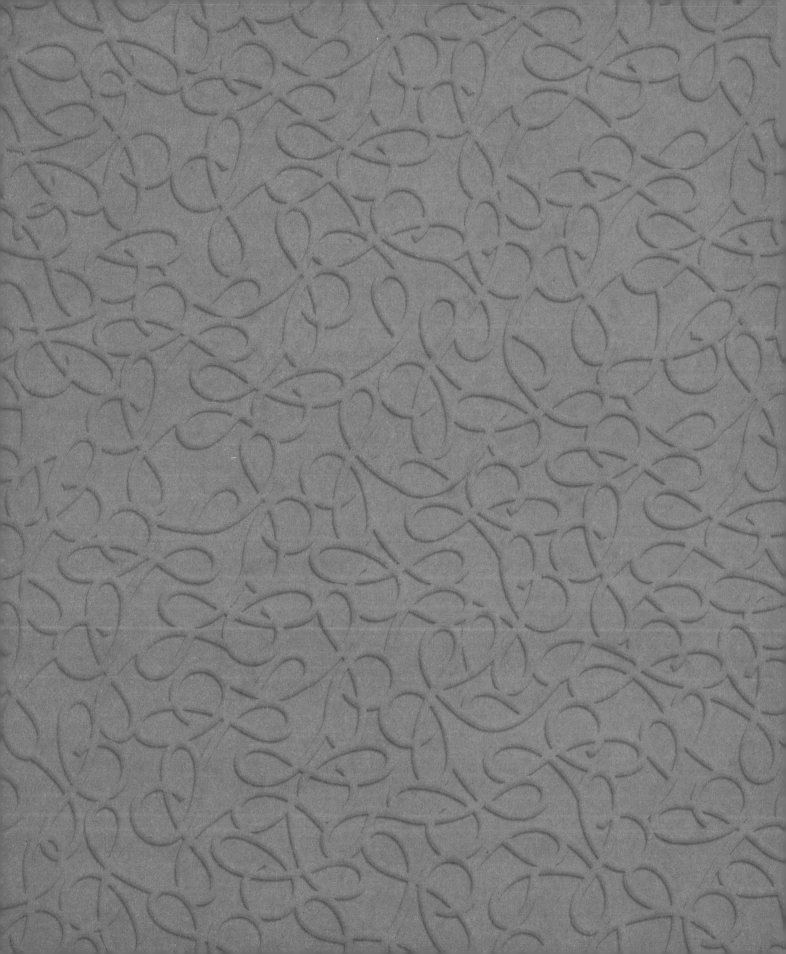

Joyful Noise

Senior Authors

Isabel L. Beck • Roger C. Farr • Dorothy S. Strickland

Authors

Alma Flor Ada • Roxanne F. Hudson • Margaret G. McKeown
Robin C. Scarcella • Julie A. Washington

Harcourt
SCHOOL PUBLISHERS

www.harcourtschool.com

Joyful Noise

Harcourt

SCHOOL PUBLISHERS

www.harcourtschool.com

Theme **6**
New Faces
New Places

Contents

Science

Science

BURTON'S FLYING CIRCUS

Science

Social Studies

Science

Science

5

6

Theme Big Books

The Thing Under
the Bridge

Decodable Books 25–30

Comprehension Strategies

Before You Read

Look at the pictures.
Think about what
you already know.

Set a purpose.

I want to find out about frogs.

RED-EYED TREE FROG

9

While You Read

Ask questions.
What do frogs eat?

Reread.
I'll read this page again.

Answer questions.
Oh! Some frogs eat bugs.

After You Read

Retell.

First, tadpoles hatch from eggs.
Then, they begin changing into frogs.
Last, they are full-grown frogs.

Make connections.

This is like another book I read.
I learned how butterflies change.

READING-WRITING
CONNECTION

	Lesson 25 >	**Lesson 26** >	**Lesson 27** >
Selection Titles	Duke's Work **Amazing Animals** The Little Turtle	Night Flight **Blast Off!** Traveling Through Time	What Brad Found **Ebb and Flo and the Baby Seal** Fellini the Fur Seal
Comprehension Strategies	Use Graphic Organizers	Adjust Reading Rate	Make Inferences
Focus Skill	Words with <u>u-e</u>	Plot, Setting, and Characters	Plot, Setting, and Characters

12

Theme 6 New Places New Faces

Burton's Barnstormers,
Jane Wooster Scott

Reading 3.1 Identify and describe the elements of plot, setting, and character(s) in a story, as well as the story's beginning, middle, and ending.

Reading 3.1 Identify and describe the elements of plot, setting, and character(s) in a story, as well as the story's beginning, middle, and ending.

13

Contents

Lesson 25

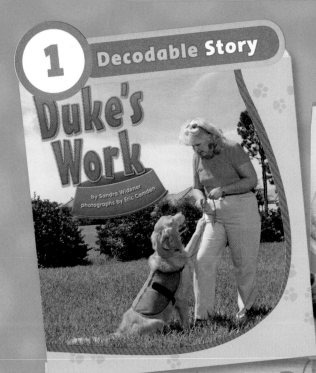

1 Decodable Story

Duke's Work
by Sandra Widener
photographs by Eric Camden

2 Genre: Nonfiction

Amazing Animals
by
Gwendolyn Hooks

3 Genre: Poetry

The Little Turtle
By Vachel Lindsay
Illustrated by Betsy Snyder

15

Phonics

Words with u-e

Words to Know

Review

love

listen

because

visitor

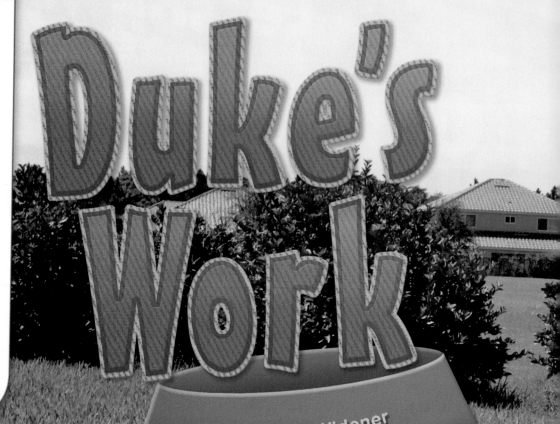

Duke's Work

by Sandra Widener

photographs by Eric Camden

16

We all love playing with cute dogs. Not all dogs are pets. A dog can be trained to help people. Duke has this sort of job.

Duke is trained to listen because Mike cannot hear. Duke hears a visitor at the door. He tugs on Mike's hand. He has just told him he has a visitor.

Some dogs are trained and used as sled dogs. Sled dogs must be big and strong. They need thick fur to keep warm.

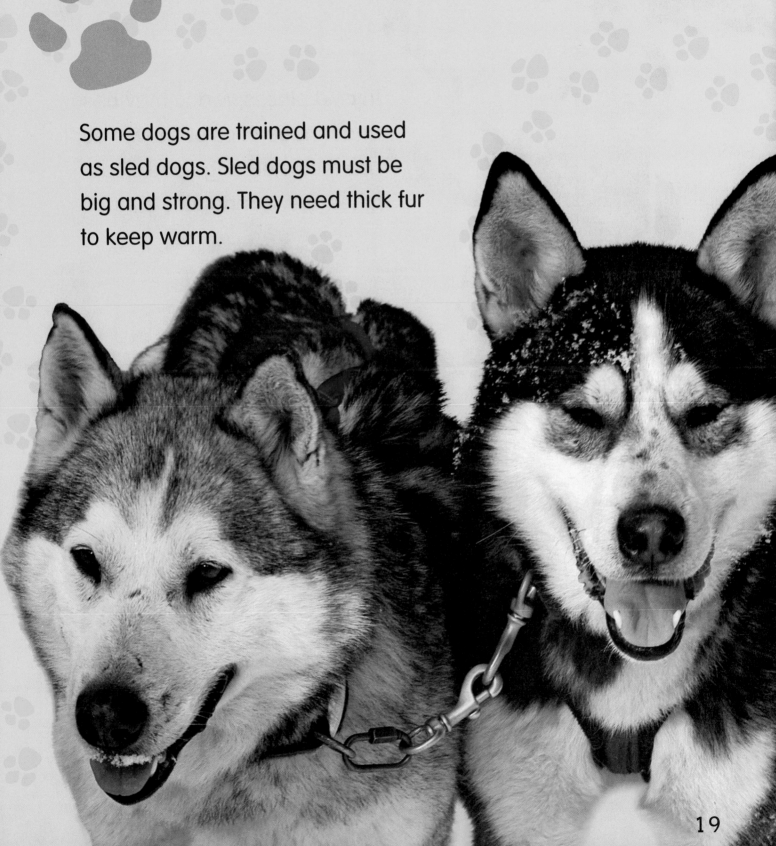

19

In cold places, roads may be lost under huge piles of snow. People use their sled dogs and sleds when they cannot use cars.

Other dogs are used for herding sheep. The herd dogs keep the sheep safe. They bark at the sheep to keep them close.

Those herd dogs make the sheep follow the rules. Herd dogs and other working dogs are used as partners and pets!

Dogs are fun, and dogs are good pets.
Dogs like Duke have jobs, but all dogs
like a big hug and lots of love, too!

Phonics Skill

Words with <u>u-e</u> R1.10

The letter **u**, followed by a consonant and **e**, can stand for the long <u>u</u> sound as in the words **mule**, **cute**, and **flute**.

mule

cute

flute

CALIFORNIA STANDARDS
ENGLISH-LANGUAGE ARTS STANDARDS—Reading 1.10 Generate the sounds from all the letters and letter patterns, including consonant blends and long- and short-vowel patterns (i.e., phonograms), and blend those sounds into recognizable words.

Look at each picture. Read the words. Tell which word names the picture.

tube

tub

tribe

cope

cube

cub

www.harcourtschool.com/reading

 **Try This!**

Read the sentences.

Bruce and June can play the flute. They know lots of good tunes. Bruce has a cute dog named Duke.

25

Words to Know

R1.11

- color
- hair
- clear
- toes
- kinds
- only
- good-bye

CALIFORNIA STANDARDS
ENGLISH-LANGUAGE ARTS STANDARDS—Reading 1.11 Read common, irregular sight words (e.g., *the, have, said, come, give, of*).

Hello! I am a polar bear. Look at the **color** of my **hair**. It looks white, but it is **clear**. I walk in the snow a lot. My **toes** are cold! I eat all **kinds** of fish. I have **only** one best friend. His name is Ice Bear. Well, it's time for me to go. **Good-bye**!

GO online www.harcourtschool.com/reading

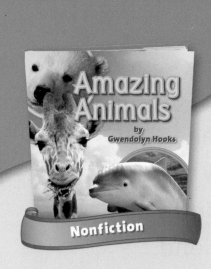

Amazing Animals
by
Gwendolyn Hooks

Nonfiction

Genre Study

In **nonfiction** the pictures and words work together to give information.

Animal	Special Feature	How it Helps

Comprehension Strategy

Use Graphic Organizers

Writing information on a graphic organizer will help you keep track of what you read.

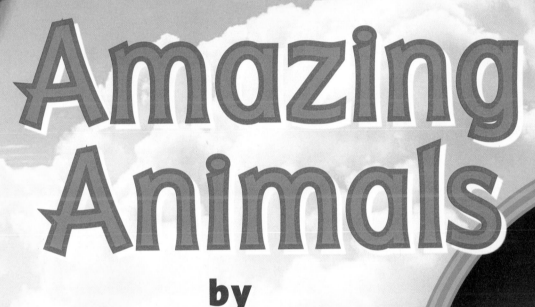

Amazing Animals

by
Gwendolyn Hooks

Big eyes, long beak, thick fur, big squeak!

Animals have many things
that help them live.

Polar Bear

A polar bear has thick fur. Each hair is shaped like a tube. The hair is clear, like glass. The sun makes it look white.

How does thick, white fur help?

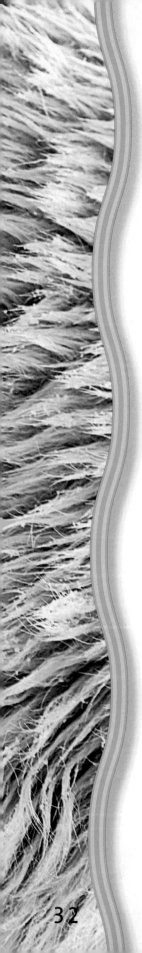

Thick fur helps polar bears stay warm.
The color of their fur looks the same color
as snow. This helps them hide.

Where is this cute little polar bear hiding?

Elephant

An elephant has two long teeth and a long nose. The teeth are called tusks. The nose is called a trunk.

How do tusks and a trunk help?

Elephants use their tusks to scrape
bark off trees. Then they eat the bark.
Elephants use their trunk to get water.

Sometimes they spray water at each
other!

Camel

Some kinds of camels have only one hump. Some have two. All camels have two rows of eyelashes.

How do humps and thick eyelashes help?

A camel's hump has fat inside. On long trips, a camel's body uses the fat for food. A camel's eyelashes keep out the desert sand.

Look at these long eyelashes!

Duck

A duck has webbed feet. Each foot has three toes. A duck has a beak, too.

How do webbed feet and a beak help?

Ducks use their webbed feet as paddles.
Webbed feet help ducks swim fast.
Ducks use their beaks to eat plants.

This duck uses its beak to clean its
friend.

Giraffe

A giraffe has spots. A giraffe has a long neck.

How do spots and a long neck help?

A giraffe's spots help it hide. The giraffe's long neck helps it reach the leaves of trees.

This giraffe is bending her long neck down to kiss her little giraffe!

Porcupine

A porcupine has quills that are long and sharp.

How do quills help?

41

Quills help keep a porcupine safe. If an animal comes too close, the porcupine backs into it. The sharp quills hurt!

What might happen to this animal?

Turtle

A turtle has a shell that is very hard.

How does a hard shell help?

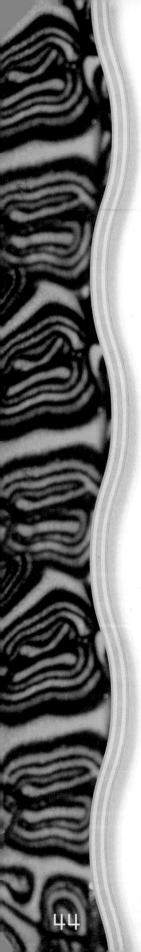

If an animal bothers a turtle, the turtle can go into its shell. When the animal goes away, the turtle comes back out.

Hello, turtle!

Dolphin

A dolphin's tail has two parts called flukes. A dolphin has two flippers.

How do tail flukes and flippers help?

A dolphin flips its tail flukes up and down to swim fast. It uses its flippers to turn to the left or right.

These two dolphins are swimming away.

Good-bye, dolphins!

Think Critically

1 Which animals have special things that help them to hide? NOTE DETAILS

2 Which animals have special things that help them to eat? NOTE DETAILS

3 What other things can elephants do with their trunks? DRAW CONCLUSIONS

4 Why do you think the title of the story is "Amazing Animals?"

MAKE INFERENCES

5 **WRITE** Which animal do you think is the most amazing? Write about it.

WRITING RESPONSE

CALIFORNIA STANDARDS
ENGLISH-LANGUAGE ARTS STANDARDS—Reading 2.2 Respond to *who, what, when, where,* and *how* questions;
Reading 2.6 Relate prior knowledge to textual information; **Reading 2.7** Retell the central ideas of simple expository or
narrative passages; **Writing 2.2** Write brief expository descriptions of a real object, person, place, or event, using sensory
details.

Meet the Author

Gwendolyn Hooks

Gwendolyn Hooks wrote this story because she loves animals. "This story is about wild animals," she explains. "I don't own any wild animals, but I do have a pet cat."

"I like writing nonfiction for children because real life is full of interesting facts.

If you want to be a writer, you should read every day. You can start your day by reading a cereal box!"

GO online www.harcourtschool.com/reading

49

The Little Turtle

By Vachel Lindsay
Illustrated by Betsy Snyder

Poetry

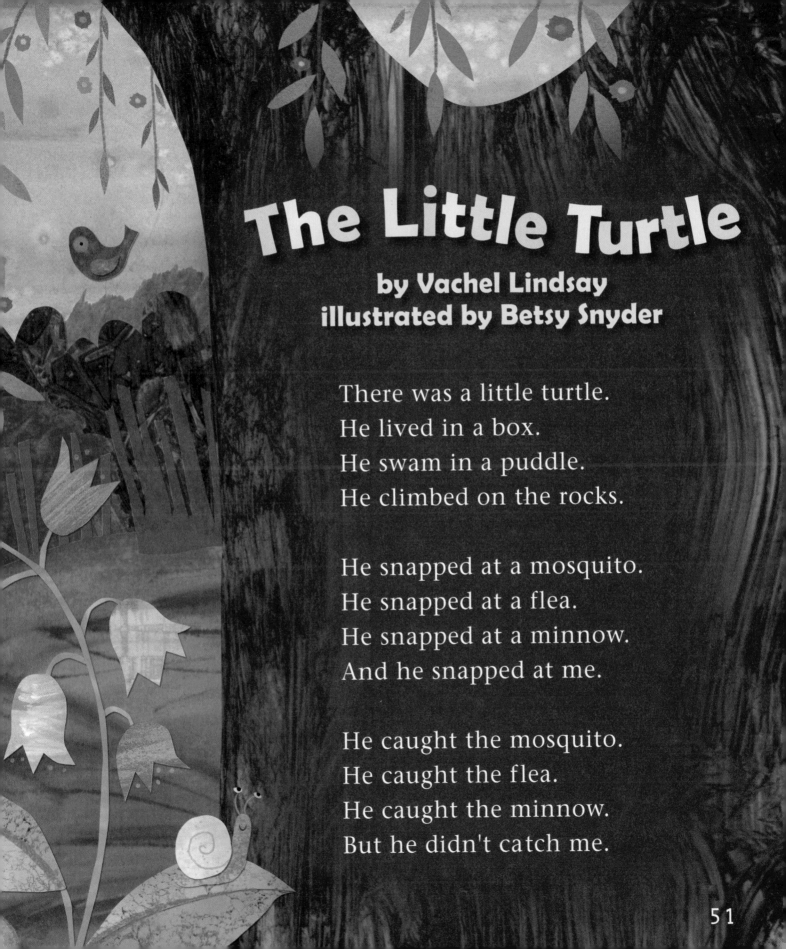

The Little Turtle

by Vachel Lindsay
illustrated by Betsy Snyder

There was a little turtle.
He lived in a box.
He swam in a puddle.
He climbed on the rocks.

He snapped at a mosquito.
He snapped at a flea.
He snapped at a minnow.
And he snapped at me.

He caught the mosquito.
He caught the flea.
He caught the minnow.
But he didn't catch me.

51

Connections

Comparing Texts

R2.2
R2.6
R3.3

1. How are the selection and the poem the same? How are they different?

2. Tell about an amazing animal you have seen.

3. What is your favorite animal? Tell why.

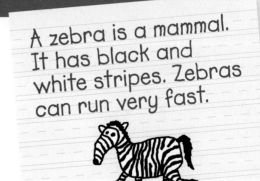

Writing

W2.2

Think of an animal you like. Look in a book for information about your animal. Write three facts about it.

A zebra is a mammal. It has black and white stripes. Zebras can run very fast.

 CALIFORNIA STANDARDS
ENGLISH-LANGUAGE ARTS STANDARDS—Reading 1.10 Generate the sounds from all the letters and letter patterns, including consonant blends and long- and short-vowel patterns (i.e., phonograms), and blend those sounds into recognizable words; **Reading 1.16** Read aloud with fluency in a manner that sounds like natural speech; *(continued)*

52

Make and read new words.

Start with <u>June</u>.

Change **J** to **t** .

Change **n** to **b** .

Change **t** to **c** .

Change **b** to **t** .

Fluency Practice
R1.16

Read the story with a partner. Take turns reading each page. Read some pages as if you are reading to a baby. Read some as if you are reading to your teacher. Listen to how your voice changes!

Reading 2.2 Respond to *who, what, when, where,* and *how* questions; **Reading 2.6** Relate prior knowledge to textual information; **Reading 3.3** Recollect, talk, and write about books read during the school year; **Writing 2.2** Write brief expository descriptions of a real object, person, place, or event, using sensory details.

Reading-Writing Connection

Personal Narrative

We have read many stories this year. "Mystery of the Night Song" is one of my favorites. Here is a story I wrote about me.

My story is called "The Painting Contest." I wrote a draft first. Then I made some changes.

Student Writing Model

The Painting Contest
by Abby

I love to paint! My dad knows this, so he got me a paint set. I painted a picture of my dog. Then I sent my picture to an art contest. I won! I was so happy.

Writing Trait

VOICE I begin by writing something that will make people want to read more.

Writing Trait

ORGANIZATION I write what happened in the beginning, in the middle, and at the end.

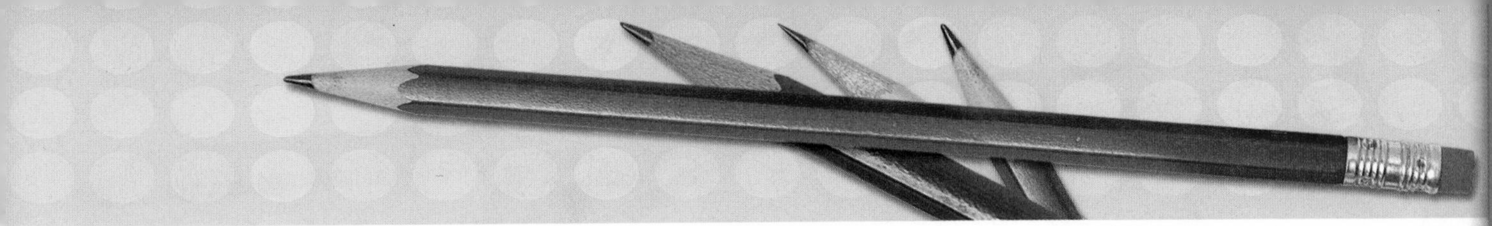

This is what I do when I write.

▶ **I write my ideas.**

camping trip

painting

visiting *my* cousins

baking cookies

▶ **I choose the idea that I like best.**

▶ **I plan my story.**

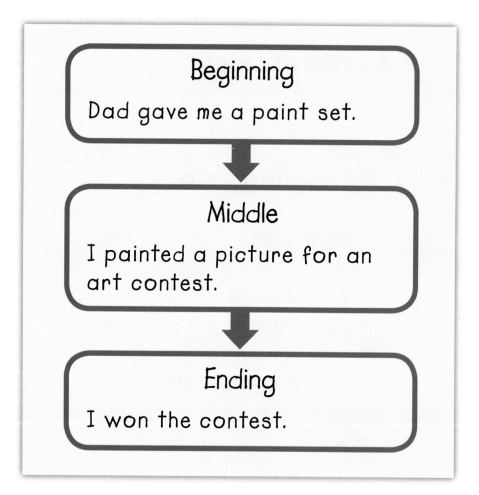

Beginning
Dad gave me a paint set.

Middle
I painted a picture for an art contest.

Ending
I won the contest.

▶ **I write my ideas.**

▶ **I read my writing and make changes.**

▶ **I type my story on a computer.**

Here are some things to remember
when you write a story about yourself.

Checklist for a Personal Narrative

☐ My story is about me.

☐ My story tells who, what, and when.

☐ My story has a beginning, a middle, and an ending.

☐ My sentences begin with capital letters.

☐ My sentences end with the right end marks.

☐ I use complete sentences.

Contents

Lesson 26

1 Decodable Story

Night Flight

by Emily Hutchinson
illustrations by Allison Jay

2 Genre: Fantasy

Blast Off!

by
Rozanne Lanczak
Williams

Illustrated by
Pete Whitehead

3 Genre: Nonfiction Article

Traveling Through Time

Phonics

Words with y and igh

Words to Know

Review

loudly

only

listen

clear

Night Flight

by Emily Hutchinson

illustrated by Alison Jay

"Fly away with me!" calls Dwight. "Let's leave
this patch. You and I will fly like a butterfly!"

"Are you nuts?" Tyrone says loudly. "We can't fly! We only have fur. We don't have wings! We can't fly like a butterfly!"

"Listen, Tyrone," says Dwight. "You think we can't fly, but I have a surprise for you."

"What might that be?" asks Tyrone.

"Come with me," says Dwight. "I'll show you."

63

Dwight shows Tyrone what he has made.
The wings are made of bright nylon. The
frames are clear and light.

"We'll take our first flight at night," says Dwight.

"What a delight!" adds Tyrone. "It will be fun.
You and I will fly like a butterfly!"

That night, Tyrone and Dwight put the wings on tight. They leap off a high hill. It is a sight to see fur in flight!

66

"Oh, my! This is not right!" says Tyrone.
"I am not a butterfly!"

"No!" sighs Dwight. "We have fur, not
wings. Oh, well! We did try!"

Focus Skill

Plot, Setting, and Characters

The **plot** is what happens in a story.
The **setting** tells where and when a story
takes place. The **characters** are the people
and animals in a story.

In the picture, the **plot** is about trying to go
to the rainbow. The **setting** is over a forest
in the daytime. The **characters** are a cat,
a duck, and a bear.

CALIFORNIA STANDARDS
ENGLISH-LANGUAGE ARTS STANDARDS—Reading 3.1 Identify and describe the elements of plot, setting, and character(s) in a story, as well as the story's beginning, middle, and ending.

Look at the picture. What is the plot? What is the setting? Who are the characters?

Try This!

Look at the picture. What is the plot? What is the setting? Who are the characters?

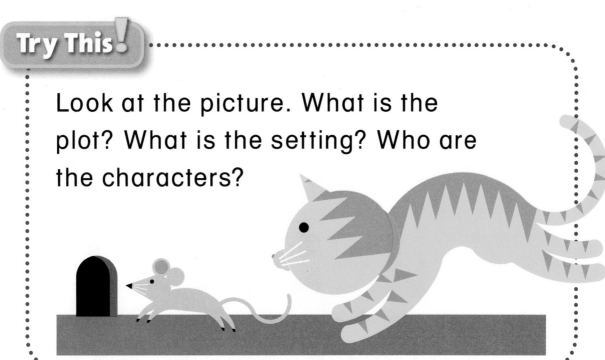

Words to Know

climbed

thought

Earth

fooling

table

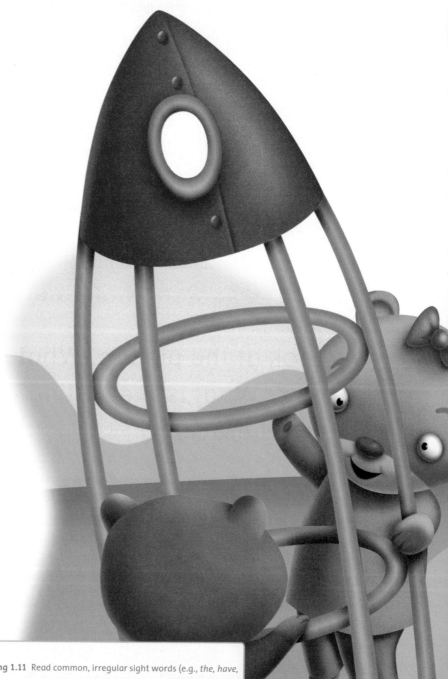

CALIFORNIA STANDARDS
ENGLISH-LANGUAGE ARTS STANDARDS—Reading 1.11 Read common, irregular sight words (e.g., *the, have, said, come, give, of*).

Kim and Tyler loved to play in the park. They **climbed** to the top of a rocket.

"I am flying to the stars!" said Kim. "Now I am flying back to **Earth**."

"I **thought** this is just a pretend rocket," said Tyler.

"I'm just **fooling** around!" said Kim. "Let's fly to that **table** over there."

"Yes," said Tyler. "Let's go!"

 www.harcourtschool.com/reading

Fantasy

by
Rozanne Lanczak
Williams

illustrated by
Pete Whitehead

Genre Study

A **fantasy** is a make-believe story. Fantasies often have animals that act like people.

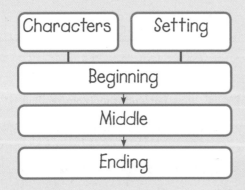

Characters	Setting
Beginning	
Middle	
Ending	

Comprehension Strategy

Monitor Comprehension: Adjust Reading Rate

If you don't understand what you are reading, you should slow down.

Blast Off!

by
Rozanne Lanczak Williams

illustrated by
Pete Whitehead

Kim and Tyler are good friends.

Their mothers are good friends, too.

One day, they all went to the park.

"I'll race you to the rocket ship!" cried Kim.

"On your mark, get set, go!"

Kim and Tyler ran. They climbed to the top.

Their mothers sat at a picnic table.

"How fast do you think this thing can go?"
asked Kim.

"How far do you think it can go?"
asked Tyler.

"Let's try to turn it on!"
said Kim.

Tyler and Kim pressed every button. They flipped every switch. They turned every wheel.

"Let's go!" yelled Kim.

"10 - 9 - 8 - 7 - 6 - 5 - 4 - 3 - 2 - 1 . . . BLAST OFF!" they yelled.

Tyler and Kim looked out the window. They left their mothers far below. They left the park far below. They left the town far below. They left the Earth and flew high into the sky!

They raced past the moon. They raced past a comet. They raced past a star. They raced to a bright green planet.

"This is cool!" said Kim.

"What a sight!" said Tyler.

"Bleeble!" said a little green creature.

"I think Bleeble means hello," said Kim.

"I think you're right," said Tyler.

"Bleeble!" said Kim and Tyler.

The two friends played with the little green creature. They swung on the swings. They jumped, skipped, and climbed.

At last, Kim said, "Oh, no! It's getting late. I think we had better get back!"

"Zight zop!" said the little green creature.

"I think that means good-bye," said Tyler.

"I think you are right," said Kim.

"Zight zop!" said Kim and Tyler.

When Kim and Tyler got back, their mothers were still sitting there.

"Oh my, look at the time," said Kim's mother. "It's time for lunch!"

"We just flew to a bright green planet!" said Kim.

"Yes, and we met a new friend there!" said Tyler. "Didn't you hear our rocket blast off?"

"Well, yes. I thought I heard something," Kim's mother said with a wink.

"Are you two just fooling around?" asked Tyler's mother.

"Bleeble!" said Kim and Tyler.

"We have a surprise for you," said Tyler and Kim.

"Where did you get them?" asked Tyler's mother.

"Look at the green feathers!" said Kim's mother.

"Zight zop!" said Kim and Tyler.
They giggled and ran off to their rocket.

Think Critically

R2.2
R2.6
R2.7
R3.1
W1.1

1 How would you describe Kim and Tyler? CHARACTERS

2 What are the two settings in the story? SETTING

3 What is the most important thing that happened? PLOT

4 Do you think that Kim and Tyler really visited another planet? MAKE INFERENCES

5 **WRITE** Write a new ending for "Blast Off!" WRITING RESPONSE

CALIFORNIA STANDARDS
ENGLISH-LANGUAGE ARTS STANDARDS—Reading 2.2 Respond to *who, what, when, where,* and *how* questions; **Reading 2.6** Relate prior knowledge to textual information; **Reading 2.7** Retell the central ideas of simple expository or narrative passages; **Reading 3.1** Identify and describe the elements of plot, setting, and character(s) in a story, as well as the story's beginning, middle, and ending; **Writing 1.1** Select a focus when writing.

Meet the Author
Rozanne Lanczak Williams

Rozanne Lanczak Williams began writing stories when she was 8 years old. She says, "If you would like to be a writer, look around you and notice things. No one sees things just the way you do. Read lots of books! That's what inspires me."

Meet the Illustrator
Pete Whitehead

Pete Whitehead says that the best part about being an artist is drawing funny-looking characters. "For me, drawing animals is more fun than drawing people," he says.

 www.harcourtschool.com/reading

Traveling Through Time

Nonfiction Article

Teacher Read-Aloud

Traveling Through Time

Long ago, people had only their feet to carry them from place to place. Now, people ride in cars, trains, boats, and airplanes.

People have invented machines that can travel on land, in the water, and through the sky. People have even traveled all the way to the moon!

Buzz Aldrin on the ▶ Moon

Look at some ways people in the past traveled.
Then, look at ways people travel in the present.

Past **Present**

How do you think people will
travel in the future?

Connections

Comparing Texts

R2.2
R2.6
R3.3

1 How are the story and the article the same? How are they different?

2 Tell what you know about outer space.

3 Tell about an adventure you had.

 ## Writing

W2.2

Think about the story and the article. Look in a book for more information about outer space. Write three facts about it.

The Moon
Sometimes the moon looks round.

CALIFORNIA STANDARDS
ENGLISH-LANGUAGE ARTS STANDARDS—Reading 1.10 Generate the sounds from all the letters and letter patterns, including consonant blends and long- and short-vowel patterns (i.e., phonograms), and blend those sounds into recognizable words; Reading 1.16 Read aloud with fluency in a manner that sounds like natural speech; (continued)

Phonics

Make and read new words.

Start with **tie**.

Change **i e** to **r y**.

Change **r y** to **i g h**.
Add **t** to the end.

Change the first **t** to **r**.

Fluency Practice

Some sentences need to be read loudly. Kim would say loudly, "I'll race you to the rocket ship!"

Look for sentences that should be read loudly. Look for some that should be read softly. Read them that way.

Reading 2.2 Respond to *who, what, when, where,* and *how* questions; **Reading 2.6** Relate prior knowledge to textual information; **Reading 3.3** Recollect, talk, and write about books read during the school year; **Writing 2.2** Write brief expository descriptions of a real object, person, place, or event, using sensory details.

Contents

Lesson 27

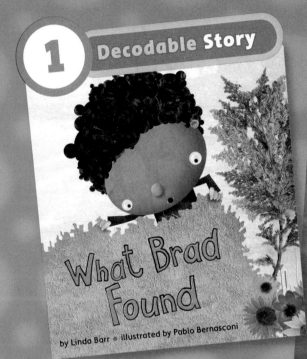

Phonics

Words with <u>ou</u> and <u>ow</u>

Words to Know

Review

hear

kinds

remembered

clear

eyes

fooling

What Brad Found

by Linda Barr

illustrated by
Pablo Bernasconi

Brad sat on the couch reading.
He set his book down.

"What is that I hear outside?" he
asked. "It sounds like crying!"

"Can I help?" he called. A big brown animal
was under the flowers.

It was a dog!

"Are you lost?" Brad asked. The dog wagged its tail a thousand times.

Brad smiled. "You surprised me!"

The dog walked around the yard. Then it raced to the house.

"Stay out of the house!" Brad shouted. Dad did not like those kinds of surprises. He remembered that Dad had made that clear.

Brad wanted to help the dog.
Maybe it didn't have a house.

Brad hoped Dad would let him
keep this dog.

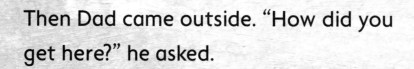

Then Dad came outside. "How did you get here?" he asked.

"Do you know this dog?" Brad asked.

Dad nodded. "She lives down the road."

"She'll have pups soon, so we must take her home." Then Dad smiled. "Would you like one of her pups? We can ask."

Brad's mouth fell open and his eyes got big and round. "You're not fooling? I can't wait!"

Focus Skill

 ## Plot, Setting, Characters

The **plot** is what happens in a story. The **setting** tells where and when a story takes place. The **characters** are the people and animals in a story.

In this picture the **plot** is about children visiting the king and queen. The **setting** is a castle in the daytime. The **characters** are the children, the king, and the queen.

CALIFORNIA STANDARDS
ENGLISH-LANGUAGE ARTS STANDARDS—Reading 3.1 Identify and describe the elements of plot, setting, and character(s) in a story, as well as the story's beginning, middle, and ending.

Look at the picture. What is the plot? What is the setting? Who are the characters?

Try This!

Look at the picture. What is the plot? What is the setting? Who are the characters?

Words to Know

High-Frequency Words

R1.11

- baby
- heard
- answered
- pushed
- pools
- together
- done

CALIFORNIA STANDARDS
ENGLISH-LANGUAGE ARTS STANDARDS—Reading 1.11 Read common, irregular sight words (e.g., *the, have, said, come, give, of*).

It was a nice day at the beach. A **baby** bird called for its mother. The mother **heard** and **answered**. The sea **pushed** a shell onto the sandy shore. The tide left **pools** of water in the sand. Two seals had fun playing **together** until the day was **done**.

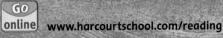 www.harcourtschool.com/reading

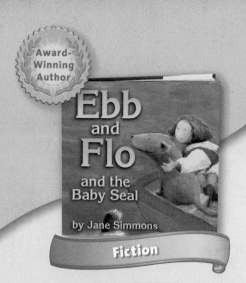

Ebb and Flo and the Baby Seal
by Jane Simmons
Fiction

Genre Study

In **fiction** authors can tell a story through what the characters say to one another.

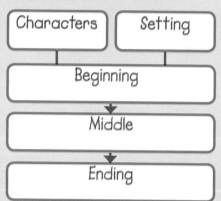

Comprehension Strategy

Monitor Comprehension: Make Inferences As you read, think about the clues that the author has left for you to think about.

Ebb and Flo and the Baby Seal

by Jane Simmons

Ebb sat and listened to the rain
and the wind.

*Pitter, patter, pitter, patter, pitter,
patter, whoosh!*

Ebb had eaten all her biscuits and
chewed her toy into little bits. She
wanted someone to play with. *Woof!*
said Ebb, but Flo was busy painting.

Woof! said Ebb, but Bird was busy chatting with the ducks.

Woof! said Ebb, but Mom was busy too.

So Ebb sat and listened to the wind and the rain.

Pitter, patter, pitter, patter, pitter, patter, whoosh!

Then she heard a cry from the beach. *Wah! Wah!*

It was a baby seal! At last
Ebb had someone to play with.
They played on the sand.

They played in the waves.

They played in the rock pools.
Ebb and the baby seal played all
day long.

As it got later, Ebb began to feel hungry.

But when she set off for home, the baby seal tried to follow.

Wah! Wah! the baby seal cried.

Ebb stopped. *Woof!* she barked.

Why wouldn't the baby seal go home?

Ebb went to fetch help.

Woof! barked Ebb.

Beep! said Bird.

"Shush!" said Mom. "We're busy!"

Woof! WOOF! barked Ebb again, even louder.

118

"What's the matter, Ebb?" asked Flo.
WOOF! WOOF! WOOF! barked Ebb
until Flo and Mom followed her . . .

. . . all the way down to the beach.

"It's a baby seal," said Flo.

"Maybe she's hungry."

"Maybe she's lost," said Mom.

Wah! Wah! cried the baby seal.

"She needs her mom!" said Flo.

"And I know where to find her,"
said Mom. "Follow me!"

Flo followed Mom, Ebb followed Flo, and the baby seal followed Ebb.

Wah! went the baby seal.

Flo heaved on the oars as Mom pushed off.

Woof! said Ebb to the baby seal.

Wah! the baby seal cried back.

They rowed all the way out to Seal Island.

Woof! Woof! barked Ebb.

Wah! went the baby seal.

There were seals everywhere.

"Oh, no!" said Flo. "We'll never find her mom!"

Ebb looked out to sea.

Suddenly Ebb saw a head bobbing all alone.

Woof! Woof! WOOF! Ebb barked as loud as she could.

Then they heard a loud *HOO!*

Wah! answered the baby seal.

"Ebb, you've found her mom!" said Flo.

The baby seal and her mother played together.

"Well done, Ebb," said Flo.

Woof! said Ebb.

Wah! Hoo! said the seals.

"Let's go home," said Mom.

130

That night, Ebb dreamed of the sea and boats and seals.

Pitter, patter, pitter, patter, pitter, patter, whoosh!

And far away there came a *Wah! Hoo!* . . .

but Ebb was fast asleep.

Think Critically

R2.2
R2.6
R3.1
W2.1

1 What is the story's setting? SETTING

2 How does Flo feel when she finds out the baby seal is lost? CHARACTERS

3 What is the problem in the story? How is it solved? PLOT

4 How can you tell that Ebb is a smart dog? MAKE INFERENCES

5 **WRITE** What would you have done to help the baby seal? WRITING RESPONSE

CALIFORNIA STANDARDS
ENGLISH-LANGUAGE ARTS STANDARDS—Reading 2.2 Respond to *who, what, when, where,* and
how questions; **Reading 2.6** Relate prior knowledge to textual information; **Reading 3.1** Identify and
describe the elements of plot, setting, and character(s) in a story, as well as the story's beginning, middle,
and ending; **Writing 2.1** Write brief narratives (e.g., fictional, autobiographical) describing an experience.

Meet the Author/Illustrator
Jane Simmons

Jane Simmons lives on an old fishing boat. She and her husband and their pets travel to many interesting places. The interesting things she sees give her ideas for her books. She uses her computer on the boat to write her books and to stay in touch with people.

 www.harcourtschool.com/reading

Teacher Read-Aloud

Fellini
the Fur Seal

Hi! My name is Fellini.
I am a fur seal.

I have lots of soft fur to keep me warm. I have flaps to cover my ears too. Can you see them? Some kinds of seals don't have ear flaps. Fur seals are special! I'm here to tell you more about us.

Fur seals live in cold places. We share our homes with other cold-loving animals. Some seals have penguins for neighbors. Would you like a penguin for a neighbor?

Mommy seals have babies in summer. Baby seals like me are called pups. When a mommy seal comes home, she calls for her pup. "Baaaa," she yells. That means "Come and eat!"

Someday I'll be as big as the daddy seal on this rock.

Now don't you agree fur seals are special?

135

Connections

Comparing Texts

R2.2
R2.6
R3.3

1 How is the baby seal in the story like Fellini?

2 What other animals could you see at the beach?

3 Tell about an animal you have helped.

Ebb and Flo and the Baby Seal
by Jane Simmons

Fellini the Fur Seal

Writing
W2.1

What if the baby seal could talk? Write what she would say to Ebb.

The baby seal would say "Thank you for

CALIFORNIA STANDARDS
ENGLISH-LANGUAGE ARTS STANDARDS—Reading 1.10 Generate the sounds from all the letters and letter patterns, including consonant blends and long- and short-vowel patterns (i.e., phonograms), and blend those sounds into recognizable words; **Reading 1.16** Read aloud with fluency in a manner that sounds like natural speech; *(continued)*

Phonics

R1.10

Make and read new words.

Start with **shout**.

Take away the ⎡**s**⎤ ⎡**h**⎤.

Take away ⎡**u**⎤. Change ⎡**t**⎤

to ⎡**w**⎤⎡**l**⎤. Add ⎡**h**⎤ to the

beginning. Take away ⎡**l**⎤.

Fluency Practice

R1.16

Read the story with a partner. Take turns reading the pages. If your partner does not know a word, give help. Give your partner a "thumbs up" for reading words correctly.

Reading 2.2 Respond to *who, what, when, where,* and *how* questions; **Reading 2.6** Relate prior knowledge to textual information; **Reading 3.3** Recollect, talk, and write about books read during the school year; **Writing 2.1** Write brief narratives (e.g., fictional, autobiographical) describing an experience.

Contents

Lesson 28

1 Decodable Story

Patty's Family Sketches
by Deanne W. Kells • illustrated by Melissa Iwai

2 Genre: Nonfiction

At the Crayon Factory
by Laura Williams

Crayons
written by Marchette Chute

illustrated by
Vladimir
Radunsky

3 Genre: Poetry

Phonics
Words with y and ie

Words to Know

Review

toes

pushed

kinds

thought

answered

Patty's Family Sketches

by Deanne W. Kells

illustrated by
Melissa Iwai

140

Patty wanted to surprise her Granny with some sketches of her family. They were all sitting in the family room. She asked each person to pose.

Dad was first. He sat by the window to feel the cool wind. He started to feel sleepy, but Patty sketched and sketched.

Mom was next. She was standing at the sink. She was smiling and posing for Patty. Her hands were soapy, but Patty sketched and sketched.

Charlie was playing ball in the backyard. He was clumsy, but Patty sketched and sketched.

Patty walked into her sister's room. Katie was
playing with her toes. She pushed them into
the air and giggled. Katie wiggled a lot, but
Patty sketched and sketched.

Lucky was under the bed. All kinds of empty treat boxes sat beside him. Lucky was happy but very messy.

"What did you do?" thought Patty, but she sketched and sketched.

Patty gave her sketches to Granny. "This is one silly family," said Patty.

"Well, I like silly families," answered Granny, "and I really like <u>this</u> silly family!"

Focus Skill

 **Details**

Details are bits of information. They help answer the questions *Who? What? Where? When?*

This picture shows many details. They tell

Who? A boy and a man

What? flying a kite

Where? a city park

When? daytime

Look at the picture. What details do you see? Do they help answer the questions *Who? What? Where? When?*

Try This!

Look at the picture. What details do you see? Do they answer the questions *Who? What? Where? When?*

Words to Know

High-Frequency Words

R1.11

great

traveled

took

able

poured

blue

almost

CALIFORNIA STANDARDS
ENGLISH-LANGUAGE ARTS STANDARDS—Reading 1.11 Read common, irregular sight words (e.g., *the, have, said, come, give, of*).

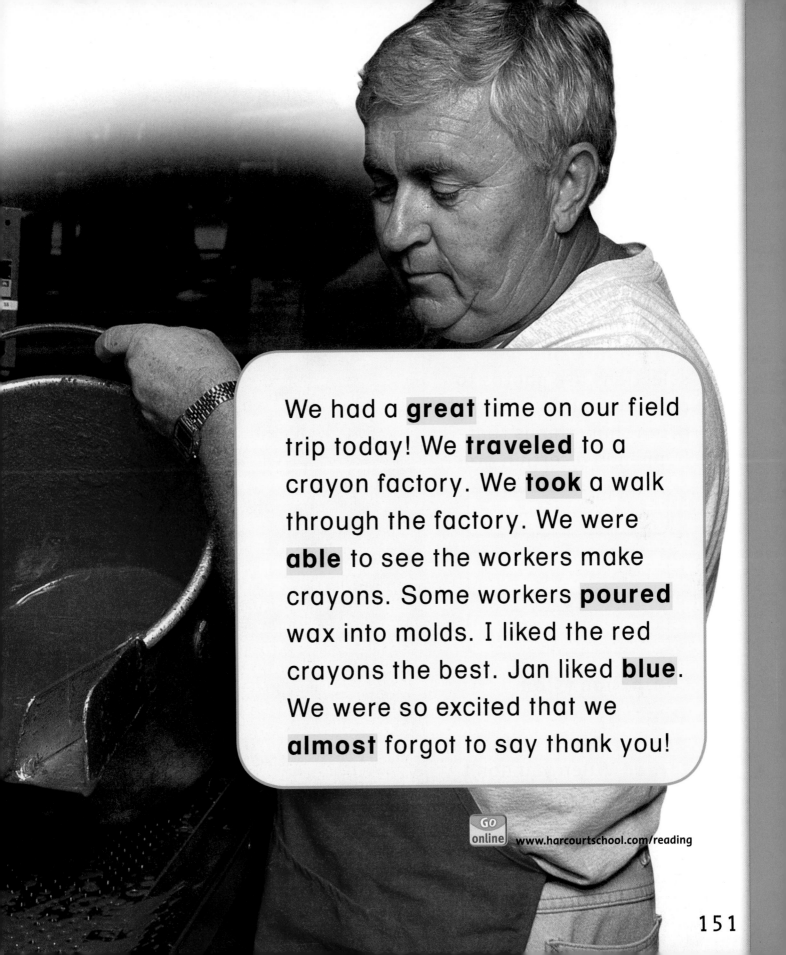

We had a **great** time on our field trip today! We **traveled** to a crayon factory. We **took** a walk through the factory. We were **able** to see the workers make crayons. Some workers **poured** wax into molds. I liked the red crayons the best. Jan liked **blue**. We were so excited that we **almost** forgot to say thank you!

GO online www.harcourtschool.com/reading

Nonfiction

Genre Study

Some **nonfiction** selections use photos to give information. They often show things that happen in a certain order.

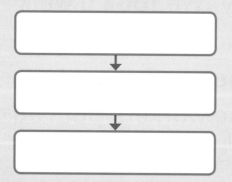

Comprehension Strategy

Monitor Comprehension: Reread When you don't understand something, read it again.

At the Crayon Factory

by Laura Williams

Look at me! I am a bright red crayon.
Come with me, and I'll show you how I was made.

It all started at a factory. First, I was part of a blob of wax. The wax is kept in some very large tanks. The tanks are very hot. Next, the wax flowed down a pipe. It went into a new tank.

Some red powder was added to the wax. Soon the wax turned red. I was very happy because red is my favorite color! The wax went down another pipe. It came out into a big bucket.

Then a worker poured the wax into a mold. The mold had many holes in it. Each hole was shaped like a crayon. Wax filled all the holes.

Cool water flowed around the mold. The water was chilly. It made the wax hard. I was almost a crayon!

A worker took me out of the mold. Other skinny, red crayons were all around me. The worker checked the crayons to see if some were chipped. Chipped crayons must be melted and made again.

At last, the worker checked me. He saw that I was not chipped. I was lucky because I didn't have to be melted again.

Soon I got my label. A machine spun me around. I was whirled and twirled. WHEEEE! I got very dizzy.

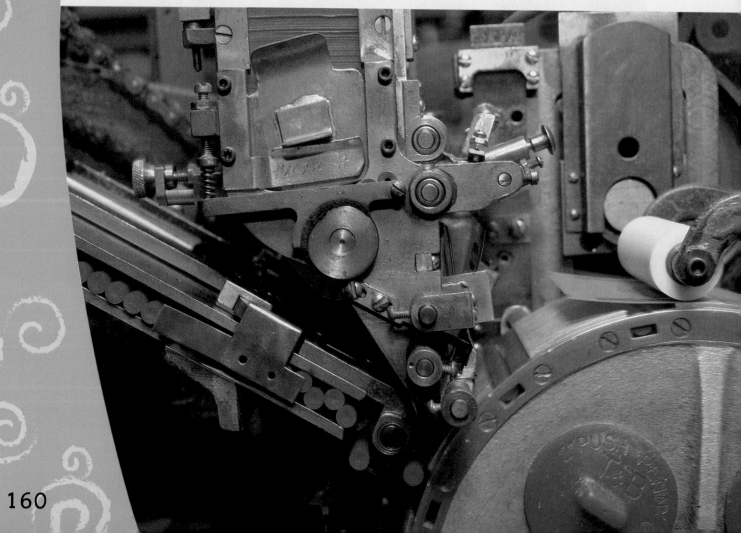

Next, a machine sorted us by color. There was
a line for each color. I was in the red line.

Then I looked down and saw some more colors.

"Hello, Yellow and Green! Hello, Blue!" I called.
"Hello, Red!" they called back. "Come down here
and join us."

Then we were all packed into boxes. Some boxes had 96 crayons. Others had 24. I was packed into a small box with 7 other crayons. All the crayons were bright and friendly. We looked great together!

All the little boxes were packed into big boxes.
Workers loaded the big boxes onto a truck.
The truck traveled a long way. At last it
stopped at a store.

A worker placed us on a shelf. "Buy me! Buy me!" I called when people walked by.

One day, a girl in a red shirt picked up my box. Her name was Kelly. Now I would be able to color something!

When Kelly and I got home, we colored some apples. The next day, we colored a beach ball. The best day of all was the day we colored a fire truck red!

Now you know how crayons are made. Think of me when you color with your red crayon!

How to Make a Crayon

STEP 1

STEP 2

STEP 3

STEP 4

Think Critically

R2.1
R2.6
R3.2
W2.2

1 How does a crayon get its shape?

🐚 NOTE DETAILS

2 Does it take a lot of workers to make crayons? How do you know? DRAW CONCLUSIONS

3 How does a crayon get its color?

🐚 NOTE DETAILS

4 Why do you think the author chose a crayon character to tell the story?

MAKE INFERENCES

5 **WRITE** How is a crayon made? Tell how you know from the story.

✏️ WRITING RESPONSE

CALIFORNIA STANDARDS
ENGLISH-LANGUAGE ARTS STANDARDS—Reading 2.1 Identify text that uses sequence or other logical order; **Reading 2.6** Relate prior knowledge to textual information; **Reading 3.2** Describe the roles of authors and illustrators and their contributions to print materials; **Writing 2.2** Write brief expository descriptions of a real object, person, place, or event, using sensory details.

Meet the Author
Laura Williams

Laura Williams has written many books for children. "I enjoyed writing this story because I learned new things," she says. "I never knew how crayons were made! I like crayons because when I use them, I feel like a child again. I like that feeling!"

Crayons

written by Marchette Chute

illustrated by Vladimir Radunsky

Poetry

Crayons

written by Marchette Chute

illustrated by Vladimir Radunsky

I've colored a picture with crayons.
   I'm not very pleased with the sun.
I'd like it much stronger and brighter
   And more like the actual one.
I've tried with the crayon that's yellow,
   I've tried with the crayon that's red.
But none of it looks like the sunlight
   I carry around in my head.

Connections

Comparing Texts

R2.2
R2.6
R3.3

1 How are the story and the poem the same? How are they different?

2 What other things are made in a factory?

3 What crayon colors do you like? Why?

Writing

W2.1

Think about a crayon that tells someone how to color a picture. Write what the crayon might say.

Pick me up and press me down on the paper.

CALIFORNIA STANDARDS
ENGLISH-LANGUAGE ARTS STANDARDS—Reading 1.10 Generate the sounds from all the letters and letter patterns, including consonant blends and long- and short-vowel patterns (i.e., phonograms), and blend those sounds into recognizable words; **Reading 1.16** Read aloud with fluency in a manner that sounds like natural speech; *(continued)*

Phonics

Make and read new words.

Start with **bunnies**.

Change i e s to y .

Change b to s .

Change s to f .

Change n n to z z .

Fluency Practice

Read the story with a partner.
Take turns reading the pages.
If your partner does not know a
word, give some help. Give your
partner a "thumbs up" for reading
words correctly.

Reading 2.2 Respond to *who, what, when, where,* and *how* questions; Reading 2.6 Relate prior knowledge to textual information; Reading 3.3 Recollect, talk, and write about books read during the school year; Writing 2.1 Write brief narratives (e.g., fictional, autobiographical) describing an experience.

Contents

Lesson 29

1 Decodable Story

A New Room by the Sea

by Deanne W. Kells
illustrated by Claudine Gevry

2 Genre: Realistic Fiction

SAND CASTLE

BY BRENDA SHANNON YEE
PICTURES BY THEA KLIROS

Shape the Seashore

3 Genre: Nonfiction Article

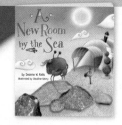

Phonics

Words with <u>ew</u> and <u>oo</u>

Words to Know

Review

climbs

almost

push

pour

great

hears

A New Room by the Sea

by Deanne W. Kells

illustrated by Claudine Gevry

Shelly has a new room by the sea. Every
day she looks at the sky. She climbs some
rocks to see the noon sun.

The sun smiles on her garden. She digs in the dirt with her new tools. Almost every flower is blooming. The yellow ones shine like the sun.

The sky is cloudy and gloomy. The wind
swirls and whirls. WHOOSH! The sea
sparkles but is not smooth. The waves
push the sand like a broom!

Now it is rainy. Shelly bends over to see pools of water pour off the roof. The sky gets dark and the wind swoops in.

It is stormy. Shelly stays in her room. She is making a warm scarf. Her eyes get droopy and she starts to feel sleepy.

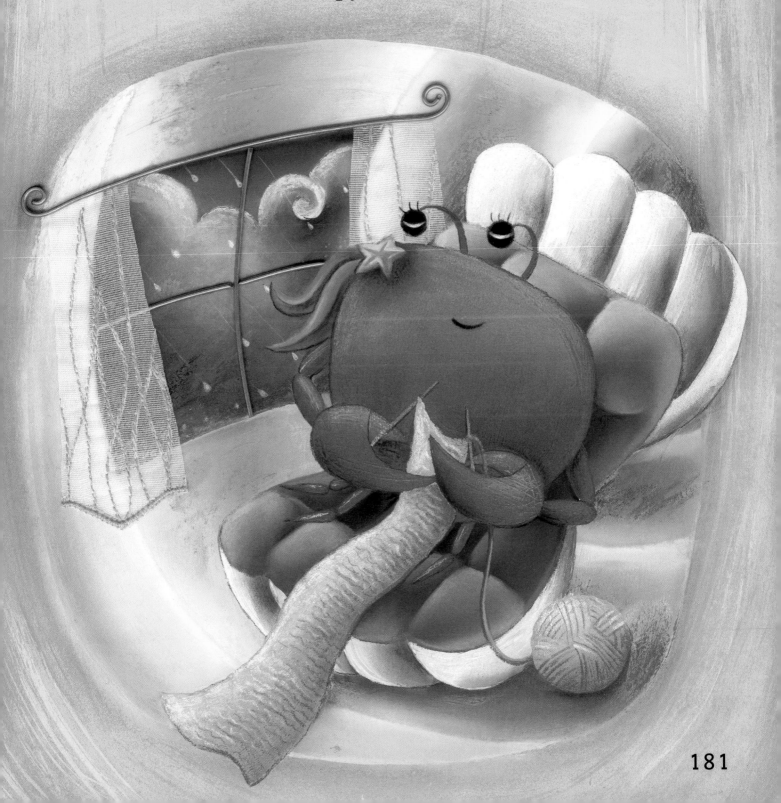

Shelly wakes up and looks at the foggy sky. She sees dew on her windows. She can see a piece of sunny sky, too. She is glad to see the sun again.

It is a beautiful day! Shelly puts on her boots and walks on the beach. She hears the sound of the waves, and she is happy. Shelly has a great new room by the sea!

Focus Skill

 **Details**

Details are bits of information. They help answer the questions *Who? What? When? Where?*

Look at the picture.

This picture shows many details. The details tell

Who? Lots of people

What? a parade

Where? a street in a town

When? daytime

184

Look at the picture. What details do you see? Do the details help answer the questions

Who?

What?

Where?

When?

Try This!

Look at the picture. What details do you see? Do they answer the questions *Who? What? Where? When?*

Words to Know

High-Frequency Words

R1.11

toward

boy

welcoming

building

tomorrow

CALIFORNIA STANDARDS
ENGLISH-LANGUAGE ARTS STANDARDS—Reading 1.11 Read common, irregular sight words (e.g., *the, have, said, come, give, of*).

This morning my friends and I headed **toward** the beach. We invited a new **boy** to come with us. Now I am making a **welcoming** sign for him. We will put it in front of the sand castle we are **building**. I hope the castle will still be here **tomorrow**!

 www.harcourtschool.com/reading

Realistic Fiction

Genre Study
Realistic fiction stories sound as if they could happen in real life.

Beginning

↓

Middle

↓

Ending

R3.1

Comprehension Strategy
Recognize Story Structure As you read, remember the order in which things happen. What happens at the beginning, in the middle, and at the end?

CALIFORNIA STANDARDS
ENGLISH-LANGUAGE ARTS STANDARDS—Reading 3.1
Identify and describe the elements of plot, setting, and character(s) in a story, as well as the story's beginning, middle, and ending.

Sand Castle

by Brenda Shannon Yee
pictures by Thea Kliros

Jen dug the sand with her shovel.
A boy with a bucket watched.
"Can I help?" he asked.
"I am building a sand castle," said Jen.
"Your castle needs a moat," said the boy.
He dug a circle around Jen's castle with
his bucket.

The castle grew taller.
The moat grew deeper.

"Can I help?" asked a girl with a spoon.
"I am making the moat," said the boy.
"This is my castle," said Jen.

"If I dig a path to the lake,
the moat will fill up with water,"
the girl said.

She scooped a path in the sand.
Water sloshed into the path and
headed toward the moat.

The castle grew taller.
The moat grew deeper.
The path grew wider.

"Can I help?" asked a boy with a cup.
"I am digging the path to the water,"
said the girl.

"I am making the moat," said the boy.
"This is my castle," said Jen.

"You will need a wall to protect your
castle," said the boy with the cup.
The boy filled the cup with wet sand.
Pat, pat. He turned it over.
Tap, tap. One sand block stood.
Pat, tap. Two sand blocks.

The castle grew taller.
The moat grew deeper.
The path grew wider.
The wall grew longer.

"Can I help?" asked a girl holding a rake.

"I am building the wall," said the boy with the cup.
"I am digging the path to the water," said the girl with the spoon.
"I am making the moat," said the boy with the bucket.
"This is my castle," said Jen.

"You need a road, so people can get to the castle," said the girl with the rake. Dragging the rake in the sand, the girl traced a winding road. With the rake teeth, she swirled wavy shapes.

Hands patted and pushed the squishy sand.

The castle rose high.

The moat dipped deep.

The path flowed long.

The wall stood strong.

The road lay wide and welcoming.

Shadows stretched across the sand.
"Angela! Time to go!"
"Robert! We're leaving!"
"Tanisha! It's late!"
"Louis! Rinse your feet!"
"Jen! Say good-bye!"

"But what about the castle?
We worked so hard," Tanisha said.
"As soon as we leave, someone
will wreck it," said Louis.

"I know what to do!" Jen said.
Splat! She jumped on the castle.
In a flurry they all kicked the road,
toppled the wall, flattened the path,
filled the moat, and crushed the castle.

"Good-bye!" the beach friends shouted
as they scattered across the cooling sand.
"Let's do it again tomorrow!"

Think Critically

R2.2
R2.6
R3.1
W2.1

1 What does each child do to help build the sand castle? NOTE DETAILS

2 How can you tell the children work well together? MAKE INFERENCES

3 What makes you think that the children have just met? DRAW CONCLUSIONS

4 What causes the children to wreck the castle? CAUSE AND EFFECT

5 **WRITE** Write about something you made with some friends. WRITING RESPONSE

CALIFORNIA STANDARDS
ENGLISH-LANGUAGE ARTS STANDARDS—Reading 2.2 Respond to *who, what, when, where,* and *how* questions; **Reading 2.6** Relate prior knowledge to textual information; **Reading 3.1** Identify and describe the elements of plot, setting, and character(s) in a story, as well as the story's beginning, middle, and ending; **Writing 2.1** Write brief narratives (e.g., fictional, autobiographical) describing an experience.

Meet the Author
Brenda Shannon Yee

Brenda Shannon Yee has been writing
stories and poems since she was a little girl.
This is her first picture book. Mrs. Yee loves
to talk about her work. She often travels to
schools to talk to children about it.

Meet the Illustrator
Thea Kliros

Thea Kliros was born in New York,
but she has lived all over the
world. She used colored pencils
and watercolors to make the
illustrations for this story.

 www.harcourtschool.com/reading

Shape the Seashore

Nonfiction Article

Teacher Read-Aloud

Shape the Seashore

Every year, artists come to the beach to build sand sculptures. People come from all over the world to see them.

CALIFORNIA

Imperial Beach

Sand sculptures are works of art. Some sculptures are tiny. Others are huge. The biggest ones may take three days or more to finish!

First sand artists spray the sand with water. Next, they pack the wet sand tightly so it won't crumble. Then they are ready to start work.

Sand sculptures can look like almost anything. Think about what you could create with sand, water, and your dreams!

Connections

Comparing Texts

R2.2
R2.6
R3.3

1 What happened at the beach in the story? What happened at the beach in the article?

2 What might you find at the beach?

3 What would you like to build out of sand?

 ## Writing W2.1

Think about "Sand Castle." Now think about another way the story could end. Write a new ending to the story.

Another ending for Sand Castle could be

CALIFORNIA STANDARDS
ENGLISH-LANGUAGE ARTS STANDARDS—Reading 1.10 Generate the sounds from all the letters and letter patterns, including consonant blends and long- and short-vowel patterns (i.e., phonograms), and blend those sounds into recognizable words; **Reading 1.16** Read aloud with fluency in a manner that sounds like natural speech; *(continued)*

Make and read new words.

Start with **boot**.

Change b to r .

Add d to the beginning. Change
o o t to e w .

Change d r to n .

Fluency Practice
R1.16

Read the story aloud with a partner.
Look for the part that begins with
"The castle grew taller." Read the
sentence that comes after this one
a little bit faster. Then read the next
sentences a bit faster still.

Reading 2.2 Respond to *who, what, when, where, and how* questions; Reading 2.6 Relate prior knowledge to textual
information; Reading 3.3 Recollect, talk, and write about books read during the school year; Writing 2.1 Write brief
narratives (e.g., fictional, autobiographical) describing an experience.

213

Contents

Lesson 30

1 Decodable Story

The Banjo Trick
by Linda Barr illustrated by Ken Spengler

2 Genre: Fantasy

Frog and Toad Together

by Arnold Lobel

An I CAN READ Book®

August Afternoon

by Marion Edey
illustrated by Maria Carluccio

3 Genre: Poetry

215

Phonics

Words with long vowel <u>o</u>

Words to Know

Review

tomorrow

traveled

answered

took

done

The Banjo Trick

by Linda Barr

illustrated by Ken Spengler

Duck was not happy swimming on his lake.
He told his friends, "Tomorrow I will look for
a way to be happy. Will you go with me?"

His friends were not so bold. They said, "No!"

Duck smiled. "I must go by myself, then."

The next day, Duck traveled for miles.
He saw Cat playing a golden banjo. "Are
you happy?" he asked Cat.

"Yes," Cat told him. "My banjo makes me happy."

"May I hold the banjo so I can be happy, too?" asked Duck.

"You can hold it for five gold pieces," answered Cat.

Duck felt so sad. "This is all the gold I have," he told Cat.

"Sold!" Cat smiled as he took Duck's gold.

"Thank you," Duck said. Then he held the banjo. "Wait! I feel the same as before."

"I don't," Cat told Duck. "I am happy to have five gold pieces."

"You tricked me! I'm done here. Keep this old banjo." Then Duck raced back to his lake.

When he got back, his friends asked, "Are you happy now?"

"Yes," Duck told them. "I am most happy when I am here with you!"

Phonics Skill

Words With Long Vowels i and o

The letter **i** can stand for the long i sound in the words **hi** and **tiger**.

hi   tiger

The letter **o** can stand for the long o sound in the words **cold** and **rolls**.

cold   rolls

224

Look at each picture. Read the words.
Tell which word names the picture.

chilled

child

chewed

gold

girl

glad

 www.harcourtschool.com/reading

Read the sentences.

Mr. Gold is a baker. He owns
the old shop over on Mild
Street. He sells all kinds of rolls and
cakes. Most people go there a lot.
His rolls and cakes are so good!

and letter patterns, including consonant blends and long- and short-vowel patterns (i.e., phonograms), and blend those sounds into recognizable words.

Words to Know

any

nothing

sorry

ready

front

226

CALIFORNIA STANDARDS
ENGLISH-LANGUAGE ARTS STANDARDS—Reading 1.11 Read common, irregular sight words (e.g., *the, have, said, come, give, of*).

"Hi, Toad," said Frog. "Why do you look so sad?"

"I did not get **any** sleep last night," said Toad. "**Nothing** you can say will cheer me up."

"Oh," said Frog. "I'm **sorry** to hear that. I'll go back home. Just come over when you are **ready** to talk. We can sit out on my **front** porch."

"Thank you" said Toad. "I'll come after I rest a little bit."

GO online www.harcourtschool.com/reading

Frog and Toad
Together

by Arnold Lobel

All I CAN READ Book

Fantasy

Genre Study

A **fantasy** is a make-believe story. It might have funny things that happen at the beginning, middle, and ending.

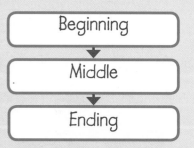

Beginning

↓

Middle

↓

Ending

R3.1

Comprehension Strategy

Summarize As you read, stop and think about what you have read so far.

CALIFORNIA STANDARDS
ENGLISH-LANGUAGE ARTS STANDARDS—
Reading 3.1 Identify and describe the elements of plot, setting, and character(s) in a story, as well as the story's beginning, middle, and ending.

Frog and Toad Together

by Arnold Lobel

A List

One morning Toad sat in bed.

"I have many things to do," he said.

"I will write them

all down on a list

so that I can remember them."

Toad wrote on a piece of paper:

A List of things to do today

Then he wrote:

Wake up

"I have done that," said Toad,

and he crossed out:

~~Wake up~~

Then Toad wrote other things
on the paper.

A List
of things to do
today

~~Wake up~~

Eat Breakfast

Get Dressed

Go to Frog's House

Take walk with Frog

Eat lunch

Take nap

Play games with Frog

Eat Supper

Go To Sleep

"There," said Toad.

"Now my day

is all written down."

He got out of bed

and had something to eat.

Then Toad crossed out:

~~Eat Breakfast~~

Toad took his clothes

out of the closet

and put them on.

Then he crossed out:

~~Get Dressed~~

Toad put the list in his pocket.

He opened the door

and walked out into the morning.

Soon Toad was at Frog's front door.

He took the list from his pocket

and crossed out:

~~Go to Frog's House~~

Toad knocked at the door.

"Hello," said Frog.

"Look at my list

of things to do,"

said Toad.

"Oh," said Frog,

"that is very nice."

Toad said, "My list tells me

that we will go

for a walk."

"All right," said Frog.

"I am ready."

Frog and Toad

went on a long walk.

Then Toad took the list

from his pocket again.

He crossed out:

~~Take walk with Frog~~

Just then there was a strong wind.

It blew the list out

of Toad's hand.

The list blew high up

into the air.

"Help!" cried Toad.

"My list is blowing away.

What will I do without my list?"

"Hurry!" said Frog.

"We will run and catch it."

"No!" shouted Toad.

"I cannot do that."

"Why not?" asked Frog.

"Because," wailed Toad,

"running after my list

is not one of the things

that I wrote

on my list of things to do!"

Frog ran after the list.

He ran over hills and swamps,

but the list blew on and on.

At last Frog came back to Toad.

"I am sorry," gasped Frog,

"but I could not catch

your list."

"Blah," said Toad.

243

"I cannot remember any of the things
that were on my list of things to do.
I will just have to sit here
and do nothing," said Toad.
Toad sat and did nothing.

Frog sat with him.

After a long time Frog said,

"Toad, it is getting dark.

We should be going to sleep now."

"Go to sleep!" shouted Toad.

"That was the last thing on my list!"

Toad wrote on the ground

with a stick: Go to sleep

Then he crossed out:

~~Go to sleep~~

"There," said Toad.

"Now my day

is all crossed out!"

"I am glad,"

said Frog.

Then Frog and Toad

went right to sleep.

Think Critically

R2.2
R2.6
R3.1
W1.1

1 Tell in a few sentences what the story is about. SUMMARIZE

2 How do you know that Frog is a good friend to Toad? DRAW CONCLUSIONS

3 Why didn't Toad try to get the list when it blew away? NOTE DETAILS

4 What makes you think that Toad is silly? MAKE INFERENCES

5 **WRITE** Write a list of the things you plan to do today. WRITING RESPONSE

CALIFORNIA STANDARDS
ENGLISH-LANGUAGE ARTS STANDARDS—Reading 2.2 Respond to *who, what, when, where,* and *how* questions; **Reading 2.6** Relate prior knowledge to textual information; **Reading 3.1** Identify and describe the elements of plot, setting, and character(s) in a story, as well as the story's beginning, middle, and ending; **Writing 1.1** Select a focus when writing.

About the Author and Illustrator
Arnold Lobel

Arnold Lobel said that when he was a child, checking books out from the library was one of his favorite things to do. He often wrote and illustrated stories to entertain his classmates.

When he began writing children's books, he sometimes got ideas from the cartoons his two children watched. Arnold Lobel wrote and illustrated many books that have become favorites of children everywhere.

GO online www.harcourtschool.com/reading

August Afternoon

by Marion Edey
illustrated by Maria Carluccio

Poetry

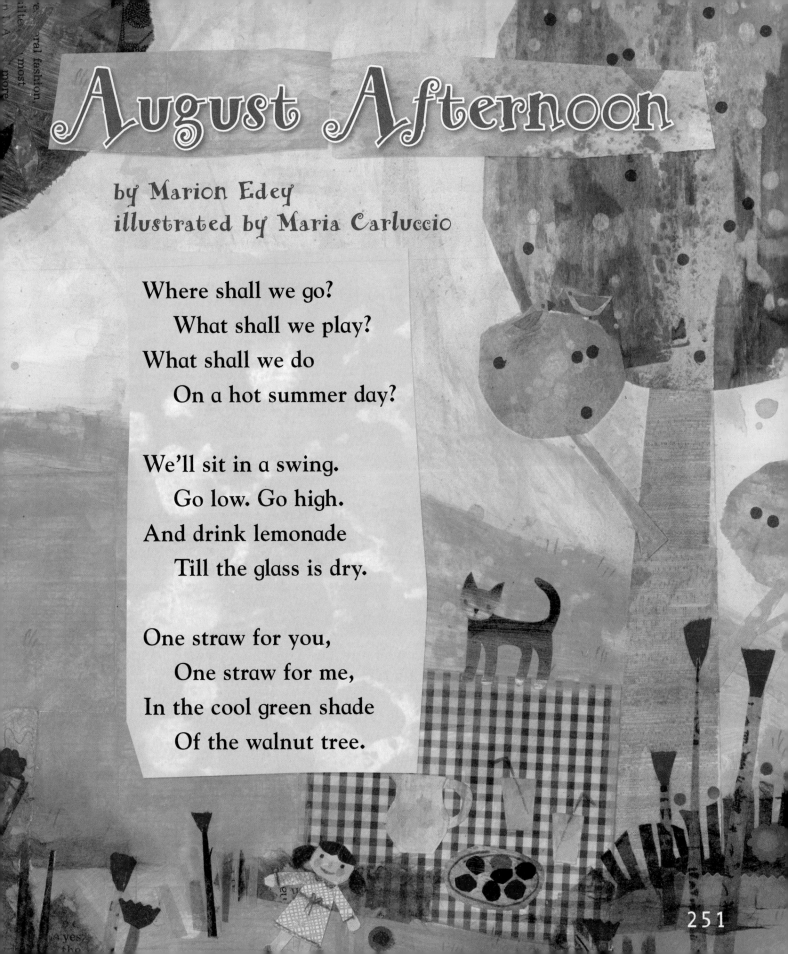

August Afternoon

by Marion Edey
illustrated by Maria Carluccio

Where shall we go?
    What shall we play?
What shall we do
    On a hot summer day?

We'll sit in a swing.
    Go low. Go high.
And drink lemonade
    Till the glass is dry.

One straw for you,
    One straw for me,
In the cool green shade
    Of the walnut tree.

Connections

Comparing Texts

R2.2
R2.6
R3.3

1 What do the story and the poem say about friendship?

2 How does doing something with a friend make it more fun?

3 What kinds of lists do you make?

Writing
W2.1

Think about how Frog helped his friend Toad. Now think about a time you helped a friend. Write a short story about it.

One day my friend asked for help. I said, "Yes I will help you!"

 CALIFORNIA STANDARDS
ENGLISH-LANGUAGE ARTS STANDARDS—Reading 1.10 Generate the sounds from all the letters and letter patterns, including consonant blends and long- and short-vowel patterns (i.e., phonograms), and blend those sounds into recognizable words; **Reading 1.16** Read aloud with fluency in a manner that sounds like natural speech; *(continued)*

Make and read new words.

Start with **kind**.

Change **k** to **m** .

Change **n** to **l** .

Change **i** to **o** .

Take away the **m** .

Fluency Practice

R1.16

Read the story aloud with a partner.
Take turns reading the pages. Imagine
that Toad speaks slowly. Read his parts
slowly. Imagine that Frog speaks more
quickly. Read his parts a bit more quickly.

Reading 2.2 Respond to *who, what, when, where,* and *how* questions; **Reading 2.6** Relate prior knowledge to textual information; **Reading 3.3** Recollect, talk, and write about books read during the school year; **Writing 2.1** Write brief narratives (e.g., fictional, autobiographical) describing an experience.

Glossary

What Is a Glossary?

A glossary can help you read a word. You can

look up the word and read it in a sentence.

Some words have a picture to help you.

write   **Jane likes to write letters.**

A
---

a•ble   Bert is **able** to see his hand in the
          dark.

al•most   The boy **almost** fell off the curb.

an•swered   The children **answered** the
             teacher.

apples

an•y   Pick **any** book you would like to read.

ap•ples   Look at the basket of **apples.**

B
---

ba•by   Josh is reading to his **baby** sister.

baby

blue

building

blue   That is a **blue** butterfly.

boy   The **boy** has a red hat.

build•ing   That **building** is tall.

----C----

clear   The sky is **clear**.

climbed   Nick and Kate **climbed** to the top of the tree.

col•or   Red is a **color**.

cray•ons   The **crayons** are red, yellow, and blue.

crayons

D
---

done   I'll call you when I'm **done** eating.

E

Earth   This shows **Earth** from space.

Earth

F
---

fool•ing   Stop **fooling** around!

front   She sits in the **front** of the class.

hair

helmet

G

good·bye   The girl said **good-bye** when she left.

great   The children had a **great** trip to the beach.

H

hair   He is getting his **hair** cut.

heard   I **heard** a tap on the door.

hel·met   He wears his **helmet** when he rides his bike.

kinds   There are many **kinds** of animals.

noth•ing   There is **nothing** to do in this empty room.

on•ly   We **only** have one pet.

pools   There are **pools** of water around the sink.

poured

quills

table

poured   I **poured** milk in Ken's cup.

pushed   The teacher **pushed** her desk to the wall.

---Q---

quills   Watch out for those sharp **quills**!

---R---

read•y   Is Dennis **ready** for bed?

---T---

ta•ble   This family is reading at the **table.**

thought   I **thought** it was time to go.

toes   She can tap her **toes.**

toes

to•geth•er   The sisters play **together.**

to•mor•row   It will snow **tomorrow.**

together

took   The children **took** their work home.

to•ward   Ray lifts his head **toward** the sky.

traveled

trav•eled   We **traveled** to visit my uncle.

Decodable Stories Word Lists

The following words appear in the Decodable Stories in Book 1-5.

Lesson 25   "Duke's Work"

Word Count: 174

High-Frequency Words

are
because
cold
door
good
have
hear
hears
listen
love
of
other
people
some
their
they
to
told
too
visitor
warm
work
working

Decodable Words*

a	help	piles
all	herd	places
and	herding	playing
as	him	roads
at	hug	**rules**
bark	**huge**	safe
be	in	sheep
big	is	sled
but	job	sleds
can	jobs	snow
cannot	just	sort
cars	keep	strong
close	like	the
cute	lost	them
dog	lots	thick
dogs	make	this
Duke	may	those
Duke's	Mike	trained
follow	Mike's	tugs
for	must	under
fun	need	**use**
fur	not	**used**
hand	on	we
has	partners	when
he	pets	with

*Words with /(y)o͞o/u-e appear in **boldface** type.

Lesson 26 "Night Flight"

Word Count: 170

High-Frequency Words

are
clear
come
don't
have
listen
loudly
no
of
oh
only
our
put
says
they
to
what
you

Decodable Words*

a	has	on
adds	he	patch
am	**high**	**right**
and	hill	see
asks	I	show
at	I'll	shows
away	in	**sighs**
be	is	**sight**
bright	it	surprise
but	leap	take
butterfly	leave	that
calls	let's	the
can't	**light**	think
delight	like	this
did	made	**tight**
Dwight	me	**try**
first	**might**	**Tyrone**
flight	**my**	we
fly	**night**	we'll
for	not	well
frames	nuts	will
fun	**nylon**	wings
fur	off	with

*Words with /ī/y, *igh* appear in **boldface** type.

Word Count: 182

High-Frequency Words	Decodable Words*		
animal	a	her	road
are	and	him	**round**
book	**around**	his	sat
clear	ask	home	set
do	asked	hoped	she
eyes	big	**house**	she'll
fooling	Brad	**how**	**shouted**
have	Brad's	I	smiled
hear	**brown**	is	**sounds**
here	called	it	stay
kinds	came	its	surprised
know	can	keep	surprises
lives	can't	let	tail
of	**couch**	like	take
one	crying	lost	that
open	Dad	made	the
remembered	did	maybe	then
so	didn't	me	this
soon	dog	**mouth**	those
to	**down**	must	**thousand**
walked	fell	nodded	times
wanted	**flowers**	not	under
was	**found**	on	**wagged**
what	get	**out**	wait
would	got	**outside**	we
you	had	pups	yard
you're	he	raced	
	help	reading	

*Words with /ou/ow, ou appear in **boldface** type.

Word Count: 179

High-Frequency Words

air
answered
cool
do
into
kinds
of
one
pushed
room
said
some
they
thought
to
toes
very
walked
wanted
was
were
what
you

Decodable Words*

a	**Granny**	**silly**
all	hands	sink
and	happy	sister's
asked	he	sitting
at	her	sketched
backyard	him	sketches
ball	I	**sleepy**
bed	in	smiling
beside	is	**soapy**
boxes	**Katie**	standing
but	like	started
by	lot	surprise
Charlie	**Lucky**	the
clumsy	**messy**	them
Dad	Mom	this
did	next	treat
each	**Patty**	under
empty	**Patty's**	well
families	person	**wiggled**
family	playing	wind
feel	pose	window
first	posing	with
for	**really**	
gave	sat	
giggled	she	

*Words with /ē/y, ie appear in **boldface** type.

Word Count: 200

High-Frequency Words

again
almost
beautiful
climbs
eyes
great
hears
looks
of
ones
over
pour
push
puts
some
to
walks
warm
water

Decodable Words*

a	happy	shine
and	has	sky
at	her	sleepy
beach	in	smiles
bends	is	**smooth**
blooming	it	sound
boots	like	sparkles
broom	making	starts
but	**new**	stays
by	**noon**	stormy
can	not	sun
cloudy	now	sunny
dark	off	swirls
day	on	**swoops**
dew	piece	the
digs	**pools**	**too**
dirt	rainy	**tools**
droopy	rocks	up
every	**roof**	wakes
feel	**room**	waves
flower	sand	whirls
foggy	scarf	**whoosh**
garden	sea	wind
get	see	windows
gets	sees	with
glad	she	yellow
gloomy	Shelly	

*Words with /o͞o/oo, ew appear in **boldface** type.

Lesson 30   "The Banjo Trick"

Word Count: 192

High-Frequency Words
answered
are
done
friends
have
here
look
said
saw
they
to
tomorrow
took
traveled
was
were
you

Decodable Words*

a	happy	on
all	he	pieces
am	held	playing
as	him	raced
asked	his	sad
back	**hold**	same
banjo	**I**	smiled
be	**I'm**	**so**
before	is	**sold**
bold	it	swimming
by	keep	thank
can	lake	the
Cat	makes	them
day	may	then
don't	me	this
Duck	miles	**told**
Duck's	**most**	too
feel	must	trick
felt	my	tricked
five	myself	wait
for	next	way
go	**no**	when
gold	not	will
golden	now	with
got	**old**	yes

*Words with /ī/i, /ō/o appear in **boldface** type.

English-Language Arts Content Standards

 **READING**

1.0 **Word Analysis, Fluency, and Systematic Vocabulary Development**
Students understand the basic features of reading. They select letter patterns and know how to translate them into spoken language by using phonics, syllabication, and word parts. They apply this knowledge to achieve fluent oral and silent reading.

Concepts About Print

1.1 Match oral words to printed words.

1.2 Identify the title and author of a reading selection.

1.3 Identify letters, words, and sentences.

Phonemic Awareness

1.4 Distinguish initial, medial, and final sounds in single-syllable words.

1.5 Distinguish long- and short-vowel sounds in orally stated single-syllable words (e.g., *bit/bite*).

1.6 Create and state a series of rhyming words, including consonant blends.

1.7 Add, delete, or change target sounds to change words (e.g., change *cow* to *how*; *pan* to *an*).

1.8 Blend two to four phonemes into recognizable words (e.g., */c/a/t/* = cat; */f/l/a/t/* = flat).

1.9 Segment single-syllable words into their components (e.g., cat = */c/a/t/*; splat = */s/p/l/a/t/*; rich = */r/i/ch/*).

Decoding and Word Recognition

1.10 Generate the sounds from all the letters and letter patterns, including consonant blends and long- and short-vowel patterns (i.e., phonograms), and blend those sounds into recognizable words.

1.11 Read common, irregular sight words (e.g., *the, have, said, come, give, of*).

1.12 Use knowledge of vowel digraphs and r-controlled letter-sound associations to read words.

1.13 Read compound words and contractions.

1.14 Read inflectional forms (e.g., *-s, -ed, -ing*) and root words (e.g., *look, looked, looking*).

1.15 Read common word families (e.g., *-ite, -ate*).

1.16 Read aloud with fluency in a manner that sounds like natural speech.

Vocabulary and Concept Development

1.17 Classify grade-appropriate categories of words (e.g., concrete collections of animals, foods, toys).

2.0 **Reading Comprehension**

Students read and understand grade-level-appropriate material. They draw upon a variety of comprehension strategies as needed (e.g., generating and responding to essential questions, making predictions, comparing information from several sources.) The selections in *Recommended Literature, Kindergarten Through Grade Twelve* illustrate the quality and complexity of the materials to be read by students. In addition to their regular school reading, by grade four, students read one-half million words annually, including a good representation of grade-level-appropriate narrative and expository text (e.g., classic and contemporary literature, magazines, newpapers, online information). In grade one, students begin to make progress toward this goal.

Structural Features of Informational Materials

2.1   Identify text that uses sequence or other logical order.

Comprehension and Analysis of Grade-Level-Appropriate Text

2.2   Respond to *who, what, when, where,* and *how* questions.

2.3   Follow one-step written instructions.

2.4   Use context to resolve ambiguities about word and sentence meanings.

2.5 Confirm predictions about what will happen next in a text by identifying key words (i.e., signpost words).

2.6 Relate prior knowledge to textual information.

2.7 Retell the central ideas of simple expository or narrative passages.

3.0 Literary Response and Analysis

Students read and respond to a wide variety of significant works of children's literature. They distinguish between the structural features of the text and the literary terms or elements (e.g., theme, plot, setting, characters). The selections in *Recommended Literature, Kindergarten Through Grade Twelve* illustrate the quality and complexity of the materials to be read by students.

Narrative Analysis of Grade-Level-Appropriate Text

3.1 Identify and describe the elements of plot, setting, and character(s) in a story, as well as the story's beginning, middle, and ending.

3.2 Describe the roles of authors and illustrators and their contributions to print materials.

3.3 Recollect, talk, and write about books read during the school year.

1.0   Writing Strategies

Students write clear and coherent sentences and paragraphs that develop a central idea. Their writing shows they consider the audience and purpose. Students progress through the stages of the writing process (e.g., prewriting, drafting, revising, editing successive versions).

Organization and Focus

1.1   Select a focus when writing.

1.2   Use descriptive words when writing.

Penmanship

1.3   Print legibly and space letters, words, and sentences appropriately.

2.0   Writing Applications (Genres and Their Characteristics)

Students write compositions that describe and explain familiar objects, events, and experiences. Student writing demonstrates a command of standard American English and the drafting, research, and organizational strategies outlined in Writing Standard 1.0.

Using the writing strategies of grade one outlined in Writing Standard 1.0, students:

2.1 Write brief narratives (e.g., fictional, autobiographical) describing an experience.

2.2 Write brief expository descriptions of a real object, person, place, or event, using sensory details.

WRITTEN AND ORAL ENGLISH LANGUAGE CONVENTIONS

The standards for written and oral English language conventions have been placed between those for writing and for listening and speaking because these conventions are essential to both sets of skills.

1.0 Written and Oral English Language Conventions
Students write and speak with a command of standard English conventions appropriate to this grade level.

Sentence Structure

1.1 Write and speak in complete, coherent sentences.

Grammar

1.2 Identify and correctly use singular and plural nouns.

1.3 Identify and correctly use contractions (e.g., *isn't, aren't, can't, won't*) and singular possessive pronouns (e.g., *my/mine, his/her, hers, your/s*) in writing and speaking.

Punctuation

1.4 Distinguish between declarative, exclamatory, and interrogative sentences.

1.5 Use a period, exclamation point, or question mark at the end of sentences.

1.6 Use knowledge of the basic rules of punctuation and capitalization when writing.

Capitalization

1.7 Capitalize the first word of a sentence, names of people, and the pronoun *I*.

Spelling

1.8 Spell three- and four-letter short-vowel words and grade-level-appropriate sight words correctly.

LISTENING AND SPEAKING

1.0 **Listening and Speaking Strategies**
Students listen critically and respond appropriately to oral communication. They speak in a manner that guides the listener to understand important ideas by using proper phrasing, pitch, and modulation.

Comprehension

1.1 Listen attentively.

1.2 Ask questions for clarification and understanding.

1.3 Give, restate, and follow simple two-step directions.

Organization and Delivery of Oral Communication

1.4 Stay on the topic when speaking.

1.5 Use descriptive words when speaking about people, places, things, and events.

2.0 Speaking Applications (Genres and Their Characteristics)

Students deliver brief recitations and oral presentations about familiar experiences or interests that are organized around a coherent thesis statement. Student speaking demonstrates a command of standard American English and the organizational and delivery strategies outlined in Listening and Speaking Standard 1.0.

Using the speaking strategies of grade one outlined in Listening and Speaking Standard 1.0, students:

2.1 Recite poems, rhymes, songs, and stories.

2.2 Retell stories using basic story grammar and relating the sequence of story events by answering *who, what, when, where, why,* and *how* questions.

2.3 Relate an important life event or personal experience in a simple sequence.

2.4 Provide descriptions with careful attention to sensory detail.

Acknowledgments

For permission to reprint copyrighted material, grateful acknowledgment is made to the following sources:

English-Language Arts Content Standards for California Public Schools reproduced by permission, California Department of Education, CDE Press, 1430 N. Street, Suite 3207, Sacramento, CA 95814.

HarperCollins Publishers: "A List" from *Frog and Toad Together* by Arnold Lobel. Copyright © 1971, 1972 by Arnold Lobel. *Sand Castle* by Brenda Shannon Yee, illustrated by Thea Kliros. Text copyright © 1999 by Brenda Shannon Yee; illustrations copyright © 1999 by Thea Kliros.

Elizabeth Hauser: "Crayons" from *Rhymes About Us* by Marchette Chute. Published by E. P. Dutton & Co., 1974.

Margaret K. McElderry Books, an Imprint of Simon & Schuster Children's Publishing Division: *Ebb & Flo and the Baby Seal* by Jane Simmons. Copyright © 2000 by Jane Simmons.

Scribner, an imprint of Simon & Schuster Adult Publishing Group: "The Little Turtle" from *Collected Poems,* Revised Edition by Vachel Lindsay. Text copyright 1925 by The Macmillan Company; text copyright renewed 1948 by Elizabeth C. Lindsay.

Photo Credits

Placement Key: (t) top; (b) bottom; (l) left; (r) right; (c) center; (bg) background; (fg) foreground; (i) inset

5 (t) Jane Wooster Scott/SuperStock; 7 (t) Jane Wooster Scott/SuperStock; (br) Jane Wooster Scott/SuperStock; 8 (cl) Digital Stock/Corbis; 12 (t) Jane Wooster Scott/SuperStock; 15 (br) Ron Chapple/ThinkStock/Superstock; 19 (b) imagebroker/Alamy; 20 (c) Hemis/Alamy; 21 (c) Jorg & Petra Wegner/Animals Animals - Earth Scenes; 22 (c) Agripicture Images/Alamy; 24 (c) Atlantide Phototravel/Corbis; (br) PhotoDisc/Getty Images; 25 (c) PhotoDisc/Getty Images; 26 (b) Wayne Lynch/Masterfile; 28 (t) Wayne Lynch/Masterfile; (b) Paul Hanna/Reuters/Corbis; 29 (r) Byron Jorjorian/Digital Vision/Getty Images; (bg) Photodisc/Getty Images; 30 (tl) Gerry Ellis/Minden Pictures; (tr) GK Hart/Vikki Hart/The Image Bank/Getty Images; (bl) Wayne Lynch/Masterfile; 30 (br) Paul Hanna/Reuters/Corbis; 31 (c) Wayne Lynch/Masterfile; 32 (c) Steve Bloom Images; (l) David Trood/Getty Images; 33 (c) Art Wolfe, Inc.; 34 (t) Thai-Images/Alamy; (l) Gerry Ellis/Minden Pictures; 35 (c) Jose Fuste Raga/Corbis; 36 (b) Gerry Ellis/Minden Pictures; (l) Kevin Leigh/Index Stock Imagery, Inc.; 37 (c) GK Hart/Vikki Hart/The Image Bank/Getty Images; 38 (t) Hans Reinhard/Bruce Coleman USA; (l) Jim Wehtje/Brand X Pictures/PictureQuest; 39 (c) Anup Shah/Taxi/Getty Images; 40 (t) age fotostock/SuperStock; (l) Seide Preis/Getty Images; 41 (c) Tom Brakefield/Bruce Coleman, Inc.; 42 (t) Londolozi/Masterfile; (r) GK Hart/Vicki Hart/Getty Images; (l) GK Hart/Vicki Hart/Getty Images; 43 (c) David A. Northcott/Corbis; 44 (l) David A. Northcott/Corbis; (b) Dwight Kuhn Photography; 45 (c) Paul Hanna/Reuters/Corbis; 46 (b) Jeff Rotman/Stone/Getty Images; (l) Paul Hanna/Reuters/Corbis; 47 (bg) Photodisc/Getty Images; 48 (bl) Lisa Hoke/Black Star; (bg) Photodisc/Getty Images; (bl) Lisa Hoke/Black Star; 49 (l) Byron Jorjorian/Digital Vision/Getty Images; 52 (t) Corbis; 59 (l) The Stocktrek Corp/PictureQuest; 90 (t) CSA Plastock/Getty Images; (br) Neil Armstrong/NASA/Corbis; 91 (tl) Dennis Frates/Alamy; (tr) Carphotos/Alamy; (cl) Corbis; (cr) Larry Fisher/Masterfile; (bl) Skyscan Photo Library/Alamy; (br) Leon Neal/Stringer/Getty Images; 93 (br) PhotoDisc/Getty Images; 95 (br) Michael Patrick O'Neill/Alamy; 106 (t) emily2k/Shutterstock; 133 (br) Stefano Torrione/Black Star; 134 (bl) Ron Levy/Global Image Group; 135 (tl) Steve Bloom Images/Alamy; (cr) Kim Heacox/Peter Arnold, Inc.; (bl) Galen & Barbara Rowell/Mountain Light; (bc) Ron Levy/Global Image Group; 137 (tr) George Doyle/Stockdisc Classic/Getty Images; 139 (b) C Squared Studios/Photodisc Green/Getty Images; 148 (c) Photodisc Green/Getty Images; 150 (c) Gale Zucker Photography; (t) Gale Zucker Photography; 155 (b) Gale Zucker; 156 (t) Gale Zucker Photography; 157 (b) Gale Zucker Photography; 158 (t) Gale Zucker Photography; 159 (b) Gale Zucker Photography; 160 (b) Gale Zucker Photography; 161 (t) Gale Zucker Photography; 162 (b) Gale Zucker Photography; 163 (t) Gale Zucker Photography; 164 (t) Corbis; 167 (tl) Gale Zucker Photography; 167 (tr) Gale Zucker Photography; (bl) Gale Zucker Photography; (br) Gale Zucker Photography; 169 (l) Mike Falco/Black Star; 172 (t) Carl Southerland/Shutterstock; 175 (bl) D. Hurst/Alamy; 184 (t) Corbis; 185 (tr) Richard Hutchings/PhotoEdit; 209 (br) Kerry Bowman/Black Star; 210 (c) Joseph Baraty; 211 (tl) Joseph Baraty; (cr) Joseph Baraty; (bl) Joseph Baraty; 212 (t) Corbis; 215 (b) Burke/Triolo/Brand X Pictures/PictureQuest; 224 (t) Joseph Calev/Shutterstock; (br) Brand X/SuperStock; 225 (tl) PhotoDisc/Getty Images; (tr) PhotoDisc/Getty Images; (br) Chuck Pefley/Alamy Images; 226 (t) Djordje Zoric/Shutterstock; 249 (br) Ian Anderson

All other photos © Houghton Mifflin Harcourt Publishers.

Illustration Credits

Cover Art; Laura and Eric Ovresat, Artlab, Inc.